Baby Animals in Their Homes

By Marla Tomlinson

Discover Plants and Animals
y as a vowel and suffix -y

Scan this code to access the Teacher's Notes for this series or visit
www.norwoodhousepress.com/decodables

NORWOOD HOUSE PRESS

DEAR CAREGIVER, *The Decodables* series contains books following a systematic, cumulative phonics scope and sequence aligned with the science of reading. Each book allows its reader to apply their phonics knowledge in engaging and relatable texts. The words within each text have been carefully selected to ensure that readers can rely on their decoding skills as they encounter new or unfamiliar words. They also include high frequency words appropriate for the target skill level of the reader.

When reading these books with your child, encourage them to sound out words that are unfamiliar by attending to the target letter(s) and sounds. If the unknown word is an irregularly spelled high frequency word or a word containing a pattern that has yet to be taught (challenge words) you may encourage your child to attend to the known parts of the word and provide the pronunciation of the unknown part(s). Rereading the texts multiple times will allow your child the opportunity to build their reading fluency, a skill necessary for proficient comprehension.

You can be confident you are providing your child with opportunities to build their decoding abilities which will encourage their independence as they become lifelong readers.

Happy Reading!

Emily Nudds, M.S. Ed Literacy
Literacy Consultant

Norwood House Press • www.norwoodhousepress.com
The Decodables ©2024 by Norwood House Press. All Rights Reserved.
Printed in the United States of America.
367N–082023

Library of Congress Cataloging-in-Publication Data has been filed and is available at
https://lccn.loc.gov/2023010425

Literacy Consultant: Emily Nudds, M.S.Ed Literacy
Editorial and Production Development and Management: Focus Strategic Communications Inc.
Editors: Christine Gaba, Christi Davis-Martell
Photo Credits: Shutterstock: Albert Beukhof (p. 7), Doug McLean (p. 10), Erica Hollingshead (p. 5),
Giedriius (p. 11), gnomeandi (p. 5), Henk Bogaard (p. 21), Holly Kuchera (p. 8), Iryna Rasko (p. 21),
Japan's Fireworks (cover, p. 17), John Michael Vosloo (p. 19), Karen Brough (p. 15),
K.A. Willis (p. 16), Kerry Hargrove (p. 18), Macrovector (covers), Max Forgues (p. 12),
Mike Laptev (p. 13), Misha Zlatarov (p. 14), Nicola_K_photos (p. 14), Roman Milavin (p. 4),
Tania Nacif (p. 20), ucchie79 (p. 9), Viktor Sergeevich (p. 14), vladsilver (p. 6).

Hardcover ISBN: 978-1-68450-686-6   Paperback ISBN: 978-1-68404-904-2
eBook ISBN: 978-1-68404-959-2

Contents

What a Baby Animal Needs

Who woke up this baby fox? He likes to sleep during the day! He yawns and then goes to play. He needs to stay close by his mom when he plays and explores.

A baby fox is called a kit.

A sleepy fox lets out a yawn.

Baby animals like to play, just like people. They may seem shy. They can be happy. Baby animals may cry, too. When you see a baby animal, its mom may be nearby.

A baby horse is called a foal.

When a baby elephant is born, it is about 3 feet tall.

Baby penguins can recognize their parents' unique sound to help find them.

A baby animal's **habitat** needs to be safe. It needs to be by food and water. Its habitat plays a key role in how they grow.

A penguin chick is born in a chilly and snowy habitat. They stay between their parents' feet to keep warm. Their fluffy gray feathers help them to stay warm.

A baby owl may have a home in a nest high in a tree or on a cliff. Other owls hatch in a nest on the ground. The mother owls try to make a nest that will be safe.

Baby owls are very fluffy, too. They are small when they are born and make a tiny hoot. They have an egg tooth on their beak that helps them hatch. It goes away as they grow.

A baby owl is called an owlet.

A Baby Cry

Why does a baby animal cry? An animal cry is just the noise it makes. It is not tears. It will make a cry when it wants something. It may be sad or happy. It may just be trying to speak.

A baby animal may cry when the mother is not nearby. It may cry when it waits for a meal or when it finds something scary.

This baby bobcat makes a big cry.

A baby bobcat may cry if it strays too far from mom. A bobcat cry is scary. It sounds like a scream.

A baby animal may cry just to make a noise. Or the baby may feel **crabby**.

FUN FACT

Humans are the only animals that cry with tears.

When a human baby cries, it usually needs something.

Baby Animals in the Forest

Many animals live in a forest. A baby deer is called a fawn. They live in forests and fields. Like all **mammals**, they feed on their mother's milk. When they grow, they eat plants and grass. Baby deer have about 300 white spots on their **coats**.

A fawn can be shy.

The mama bear looks on as her cubs play.

Baby bears are called cubs. Bear cubs are born in winter, while their mother is **hibernating**. They keep toasty warm as they sleep cuddled on their mom's furry belly.

Bears live in dens in the forest. In spring they come out to explore and play. They play fight and learn how to find food.

11

Learn to Fly

We can see birds fly in the sky all over the world. Baby birds need to learn to fly. At first they stay safe in their nest. They make a squeaky cry when they want food to eat. They rely on their mother to bring them food.

These baby birds cry for food.

In a few weeks, the **hatchlings** try to fly. They learn to fly by watching their parents and by practicing. Most birds don't fly on their first try. They may fall or not take off. When a baby bird starts to flap its wings, it is ready to learn to fly.

This baby bird may try to fly soon.

Stages of a Baby Bird

Birds grow fast. Most need to grow their feathers to fly. Below are the stages of baby birds who are born in a nest.

Hatchling – Just hatched. It may not have feathers and its eyes are closed.	
Nestling – Still growing in the nest.	
Fledgling – Starting to learn to fly.	

A Baby in a Pocket

Imagine being only one inch tall when you were born. That is very tiny! But that's how small a kangaroo is when it is born. The tiny baby kangaroo is called a joey.

The baby is so small and weak that it is not safe. To be safe, the baby kangaroo climbs up its mother and stays inside a pouch on her belly. This pouch is like a pocket for the baby. The joey will grow there until it is bigger and ready to hop out and play.

The baby kangaroo habitat is mostly found in hot and dry grassy areas.

Kangaroo joeys grow from just one inch to between three and eight feet.

Animals with pouches for their babies to grow in are called marsupials. Some marsupials do not have a pouch. But these babies still hold on to their mother until they are bigger.

Each marsupial baby is called a joey. They like the heat. They live in hot places like Australia.

This baby kangaroo takes a ride in its mama's pouch.

Koalas are marsupials. You would meet them in their home high in the trees. This is near the leaves they eat. A koala joey stays safe in its mother's pouch and she stays safe up in the treetops.

A baby koala stays in the pouch until it is about six months old. Then it rides on its mother's back or clings to her tummy to keep safe.

FUN FACT

Koalas sleep 18 hours a day. They can snooze while holding tight to a branch high in a tree.

This joey is too big to ride in the pouch so it rides on its mother's back.

Ready to Go

Many animals need to be ready to try to stand and walk soon after they are born.

A mountain goat baby is called a kid. Mountain goats live in an **alpine** habitat. This habitat is snowy and rocky. They need to try to stand right away to be safe. They don't want to fall! They need to run. They learn fast about how to make their way on the rocks.

These kids try to jump and play on the rocks.

A giraffe's neck can be six feet long.

What about the tall giraffe? They are six feet tall when they are born and weigh about 150 pounds! A baby giraffe is called a calf. They also need to be ready to walk and run within hours of being born. This is because they share a habitat with **predators** like lions. They may need to be sneaky and flee!

Water Baby

What about baby animals born in a water habitat?

Baby sharks, called pups, are born in shallow water so they have lots of food nearby. They make their way to deep water when it is safer for them.

FUN FACT

The blue whale baby is born one of the biggest animals on Earth. It is about 5,000 pounds at birth and over 20 feet long!

Baby sea turtles hatch without parents. They are born on dry land. The mother lays the eggs on the beach and leaves. A sandy sea turtle makes its way to its water habitat after being born.

This baby sea turtle makes its way through the sand.

Baby Animals at Home

All animals start out as babies. They need to learn and grow, just like we do. Their play is a way to learn and try new things.

Happy or crabby, baby animals are safest near their habitats and home. It has what they need to live and grow.

These baby lions like to play!

These monkeys hold on to their babies to keep them safe.

Glossary

alpine: mountain area

coats: animals' fur

crabby: unhappy, annoyed

habitat: the natural place where an animal or plant lives

hatchlings: baby birds just after they hatch from their egg

hibernating (hī-bər-nā-ting): when an animal is resting in winter to save energy

mammals: animals that give their milk to their babies

predators (prĕd -ŭ-tərs): animals that rely on other animals for food

Index

Vowel Teams

vowel -y

baby	by	dry	rely	try
belly	cry	only	shy	why

suffix -y

chilly	fluffy	happy	scary	sneaky	squeaky
crabby	furry	sandy	sleepy	snowy	toasty

High-Frequency Words

after	does	mother	only	sound(s)	want
animal	learn	new	over	through	world
away	live	old	small	very	
because	most				

Challenging Words

climbs	fledgling	many	noise	pouch	weigh
fawn	giraffe	marsupials	penguin	pounds	yawns
feathers	grow	mountain	people		
fields	imagine				